SAVING SEA OTTERS

STORIES OF SURVIVAL

ELIN KELSEY WITH PHOTOGRAPHS BY DOC WHITE

MONTEREY BAY AQUARIUM PRESS

MONTEREY, CALIFORNIA

The mission of the Monterey Bay Aquarium
is to inspire conservation of the oceans.

To the memory of Margaret Wentworth Owings and her commitment to sea otters and other wildlife.

ACKNOWLEDGMENTS

These stories would not exist were it not for the inspiring work of the SORAC staff and volunteers. Special thanks to: Andy Johnson, Michelle Staedler, Julie Hymer, Sue Campbell, Candice Tahara, Twyla Anderson, Katie Hawkins, Karl Mayer, Teri Nicholson, Greta Kay Austin, and to Tom Williams who founded and provided leadership to the program for its first decade. Dozens of volunteers contribute to the SORAC program. We would like to extend our appreciation to Karen Drayer, Kim Beals, Peggy Miars, Jennifer Pavlett, Marsha Malis, Jean Matthias Breheney, Chris Miller, Jeannette Post, Joanne Flanders and Peggy Young, for sharing their personal experiences as volunteers. We would also like to thank the sea otter husbandry staff: Michelle Jeffries, Michelle Sousa, Alisa Giles and Kacey Kurimura.

The SORAC program operates in collaboration with an incredible network of organizations and individuals. We would like to thank: Mike Murray of the Avian and Exotic Clinic of the Monterey Peninsula; Jim Curland of the Friends of the Sea Otter; Billy Hurley and Heather Norman of the Long Marine Lab; Dave Jessup, Jack Ames and Mike Harris of the California Department of Fish and Game; Brian Hatfield of the United States Geological Survey; Jim Estes of the University of California, Santa Cruz; Melissa Chechowitz, Pat Conrad and Krista Hanni of the University of California, Davis; Nancy Kock of The Marine Wildlife Veterinary Care and Research Center; Larry White of Monterey Bay Youth, and the organizers of the Seattle sea otter workshop, for their insights and assistance.

Stories become a book through the hard work of many. Many thanks to Betty Watson for her stunning book design; to Julie Packard, Chris Harrold, Mike Murray and Andy Johnson for their thoughtful review of the manuscript; to Cristina Fekeci and Ken Peterson for their support of this project; to Nora Deans for her editorial guidance and her tireless efforts to bring this book to press, and to Roxane Buck-Ezcurra and Michelle McKenzie for their smooth handling of the editorial process.

Thanks to one and all for your support, friendship and professionalism.

—EK and DW

And, to my husband Andy, warmest thanks for your loving support and stimulating debates. You are my foil.

—EK

Special thanks go to my wife, Ceci Devereaux White, to my friend Steve Drogin and to skipper Ed Cooper. I am grateful to my friend Rich Gallangher for donating his boat.

—DW

There is something about sea otters that captures our hearts. Maybe it's the way a mother otter cuddles her sleeping pup, or the way a pup cries when it's left alone on the surface while its mother dives for food. Maybe it's the way sea otters busily groom their fur, or lazily doze in the kelp beds.

Whatever it is, these engaging animals give people an emotional connection to the health of the ocean environment. And the plight of the southern sea otter— its population declining to the point that it could soon become an endangered species—offers a warning signal that something is seriously wrong.

At the Monterey Bay Aquarium, our mission is to inspire conservation of the oceans. We're also actively engaged in ocean conservation initiatives including, since 1984, our Sea Otter Research and Conservation program. Through our work with sea otters, we've learned how to rescue injured and orphaned animals, and to return them successfully to the wild. We've gained valuable skills that can be applied to emergency rescue efforts for large numbers of sea otters in the event of an oil spill or other environmental catastrophe. And we've built relationships with colleagues who are also working for the survival of the sea otter.

This book is a window into the world of the sea otter, and that of the people who work with them—a committed group of staff and volunteers who labor around the clock on behalf of sea otters and healthy oceans. I hope you'll find their stories inspiring—a starting point for your own further involvement in ocean conservation.

The challenges of protecting sea life for future generations are great. They will take the best efforts that each of us can muster. But there is no more important work before us. Our survival, and the survival of all life on Earth, depends on healthy oceans. Sometimes you contribute by writing a letter to a legislator, sometimes by walking to the store instead of taking a car. You can help by working with ocean wildlife, or by supporting programs like our Sea Otter Research and Conservation efforts here at the aquarium.

I hope the story of sea otters will encourage you to become more active on behalf of our oceans and the remarkable life they sustain. That way, each time you see a sea otter in the wild, or in a photo, book or film, you'll know that you did your part to preserve a world where sea otters will always have a place.

Julie Packard

Executive Director, Monterey Bay Aquarium

CONTENTS

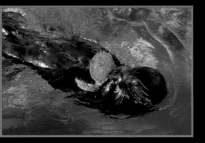

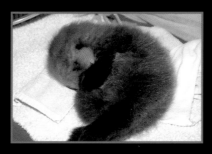

INTRODUCTION

On a clear, sunny day when the Pacific stretches flat and lazy before you, it's easy to envy the sea otters in Monterey Bay. Here, amid the shimmering golden kelp, they rest and feed and groom, groom, groom in an endless cycle of day and night. Sea otters are so visible, so ever present along the harbors and beaches and rocky shores of this spectacular peninsula, you can follow the details of their lives from the comfort of a patio restaurant. Unlike marine mammal watching in most places on Earth, sea otter viewing and fine dining coexist in Monterey Bay—the "crack" of an otter pounding a clamshell mixing with the clink of glasses and the scraping of plates.

But there's another side to this tranquil scene. The sea otters that roll and dive and tumble along this magical coastline are, in reality, rare. You'd find more students in an average high school than you would southern sea otters in the entire world. Numbering slightly more than 2,000 individuals, the southern sea otter population is classified as a threatened species. And recent surveys confirm

what many have feared: the population of southern sea otters is declining.

Can southern sea otters be saved? This book is about the sea otters of California, and a group of women and men committed to their survival. The sensitive portraits that follow provide an intimate glimpse into a wildlife conservation program as rare as the animals it serves. There is no recipe for helping a sea otter pup survive the first traumatic days following an initial stranding. Raising it to be a healthy juvenile is more challenging still. But, pioneering effective ways to rear sea otters for successful integration into the wild is the toughest challenge of all. Every sea otter that passes through the Monterey Bay Aquarium's Sea Otter Research and Conservation (SORAC) program is rehabilitated for return to the wild. While it is not always possible to achieve this extraordinarily difficult goal, the Monterey Bay Aquarium's record of success is unparalleled.

The SORAC program is an ongoing experiment in the human capacity to save animals in peril. For the past fifteen years, this unique conservation initiative has been quietly and steadily rehabilitating orphaned and injured sea otters and tracking their survival back at sea. It's a program where diving with an orphaned sea otter pup on a warm summer's day goes hand-in-hand with tracking a radio-tagged adult through a muddy marsh in a rainstorm. It's a program where the ability to make a "clam shake" is ranked as highly as one's skill at identifying flipper tags from a pitching boat in high seas, or quieting a restless pup on the midnight to six shift. And for the dozens of volunteers and staff who make this endeavor a reality, it's a testament to the belief that the greatest reward for countless hours of effort and caring comes when the sea otter that depended on you for everything is now thriving in the wild without you.

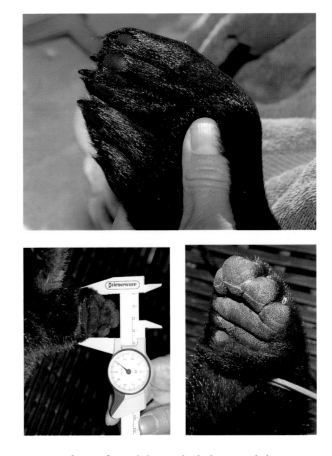

◄ ▲ *Vast forests of giant kelp provide ideal sea otter habitat just beyond the Monterey Bay Aquarium's doors.*

◄ *Kelp from a sea otter's natural habitat helps this orphaned pup feel more secure at the aquarium.*

▲ ▲ *Sea otters use the sharp claws on their hind flippers to groom their incredibly thick fur.*

▲ *Paw measurements allow researchers to determine the size of sea otter's prey. If they spot an adult otter eating a "two paw" cancer crab through their binoculars, for example, they can estimate the crab's size to be eight to ten centimeters.*

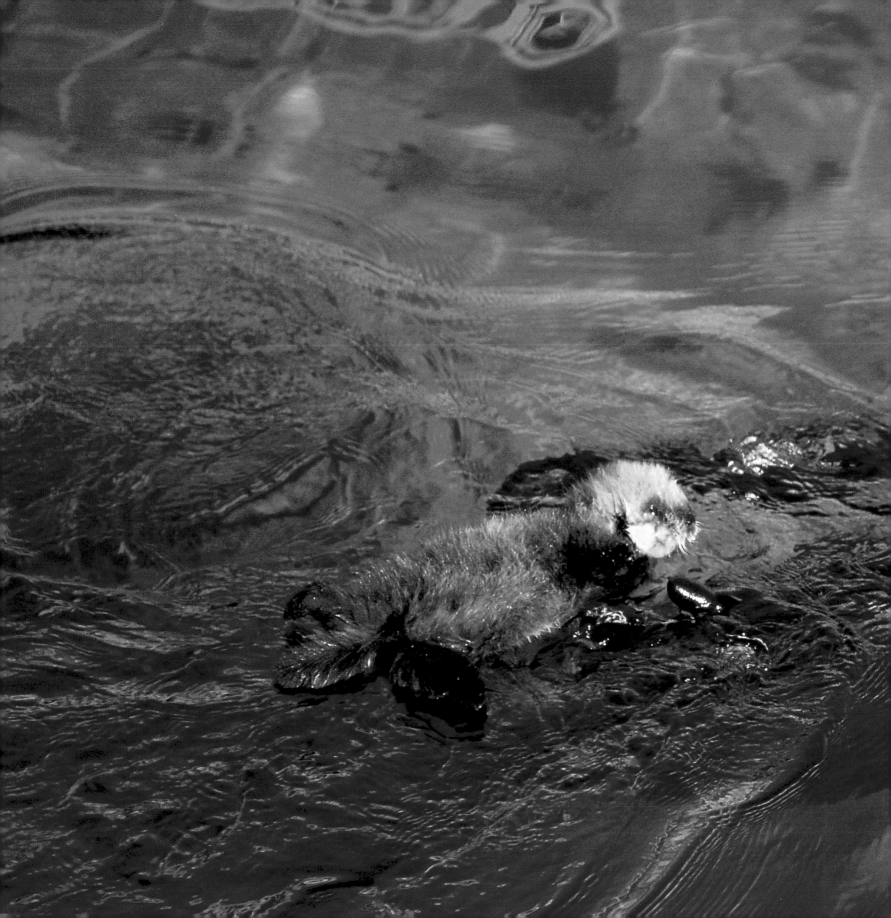

RESCUE AND CARE

PUP CARE

Playing Musical Totes at 3:00 A.M.

■ *When a sea otter pup is found alone on a beach there is little question that it has lost its mother and is desperately in need of alternative care.*

◄ A five-week-old orphaned pup looks to a SORAC diver for reassurance during an ocean swim.

▲ Daily weigh-ins enable SORAC staff and volunteers to monitor pup growth and development.

► Twenty-four hours of snuggling, swimming, grooming and drying young sea otters creates an impressive laundry load—five washer loads per pup per day!

►► No other animal on Earth is as soft and fluffy as a newborn sea otter pup.

Playing Musical Totes at 3:00 A.M.

Big Sur is renowned for two things—stunning coastal scenery and the largest rural marathon on Earth. Each spring, thousands of runners from all over the world journey to this wild coast to experience 26.2 miles of challenging hills and sweeping ocean views. The arduous two-mile ascent to Hurricane Point in headwinds is a test for even the fittest of athletes. But when it comes to sheer endurance, it is the newborn sea otter pup bobbing in the surf far beyond the view of the runners that takes the honors.

Observing baby sea otters in the wild is not for the faint of heart. A three-pound package of fluff appears totally ill-suited for birth into an aquatic environment where storm waves can reach 30 feet high and water temperatures may drop to 45 degrees Fahrenheit. Yet, if you can muster enough courage to

◄ *During its first weeks of life, a sea otter pup is totally dependent upon its caregivers.*

◄▲ *Bottle feeding is an ideal way to administer nutritional supplements to a hand-raised juvenile experiencing health problems.*

▲ *SORAC staff and volunteers do their best to mimic the close bond between a wild sea otter mother and pup.*

▲ *The fleece covering this bottle is just one of many innovative devices caregivers have developed to increase the pup's comfort and decrease its association with artificial objects.*

▶ *Sea otters grow so quickly that by the time this young male is eight weeks old, he'll be too large to fit this scale.*

train your binoculars in close for a look, you'll discover a miraculous sight. The pup is sleeping! Through rolling breakers and white-capped swells, it rides this turbulent sea like a babe in a rocker. Birth at sea, nurse at sea, mate at sea, and eventually, die at sea: these smallest of marine mammals spend their entire lives in the ocean. So, when a sea otter pup is found alone on a beach there is little question that it has lost its mother and is desperately in need of alternative care.

I am thinking of how difficult it must be to prepare a pup for a life of such epic demands, as I look around the conference room at the SORAC volunteers. My husband, Andy, manages the SORAC program; and as a writer and spouse I've been treated to an insider's view of the program in action. Yet, I still find myself wondering how a group of humans, no matter how well-intentioned, can fill the role of a sea otter mother. "We can't," Julie, the woman who coordinates the stranding program, assures me. "There is simply no way we can lay on our backs in sea water and nurse them and lick their fur 24 hours a day. Rehabilitation is not natural, it's not the way an otter pup is supposed to grow up. But that doesn't mean it isn't effective. It's a long, slow process of assessing each individual pup's needs and giving it the care, food, grooming, security and experience it needs to grow healthy and strong."

"A sea otter pup has one mother in the wild. So, when a pup first arrives, we try to cover its twenty-four-hour care by having two people each work a twelve-hour shift. As the pup becomes more comfortable, we'll increase the number of people who are able to care for it and decrease the length of each shift. By a few weeks of age, a pup may have ten to twelve 'moms,' or caregivers, each with his or her own style of holding, feeding, brushing and playing. We

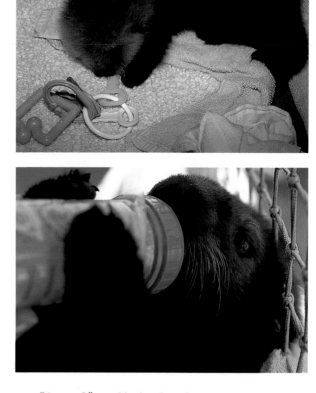

▲ ▲ *"Otter safe" toys, like this plastic key ring, help sooth teething pups.*

▲ *Notice how much shorter and sleeker the fur of this six-month-old juvenile is from the five-week-old pup in the photo above.*

▲ ▲ *Nail brushes, tooth brushes, eyebrow brushes, flea combs—utensils of all sizes are used to penetrate and groom the thick layers of a young sea otter's coat.*

▲ *A clam adductor muscle is no match for the impressive teeth of this six-month-old sea otter.*

▶ *Wet on the outside, dry on the inside . . . water beads down the outer guard hairs of this juvenile, ensuring that his soft undercoat stays warm and dry.*

agree as a team on the way the pup will be raised, but there are individual judgments that caregivers must make every step of the way."

It sounds idyllic: twelve hours of uninterrupted time playing nursemaid to one of the most charming creatures on Earth. "I've never been so excited to stay up all night," a volunteer tells me. "I fed him his bottle and held him while he slept and played 'wet towel' for forty minutes. He rode through the water on it, attacked it from under the haulout and held onto it while I 'dunked' him. I'll never forget those precious moments at 3:00 a.m."

"Pups need a lot of handling, a lot of stimulation and personal attention when they're young," Julie explains as she blends squid, clams, half-and-half cream and various vitamins and minerals into a batch of sea otter formula. "Our biggest challenge is finding the best way to hand-raise each individual so that it can be successfully introduced into the wild population. We don't want these animals to grow up to be social outcasts. We want them to play, feed, groom, socialize and, ultimately, reproduce, just as well as a sea otter raised by its mother. That's an incredibly ambitious goal."

The Monterey Bay Aquarium's rehabilitation program is fifteen years old. It is the world's most sophisticated program in terms of rehabilitating sea otters for release, yet Julie and her teammates believe strongly that the program is only in its kindergarten phase. "We still haven't had a perfect case," Julie declares. But dozens of pups have passed through the program and returned to the sea thanks to SORAC care. In my mind, that deserves a graduation ceremony.

HUSBANDRY

Clamsicles and Hair Clogs

■ It's a long, slow process of assessing each individual pup's needs and giving it the care, food, grooming, security and experience it needs to grow healthy and strong.

▲ A tube pipe filled with frozen clams provides a stimulating feeding challenge for this young female.

▶ A juvenile male effortlessly bends his foot to his chest. Such amazing flexibility enables a sea otter to groom every square inch of its body.

▶▶ A juvenile sea otter must be able to catch, open and eat a live crab before it can be released to the wild.

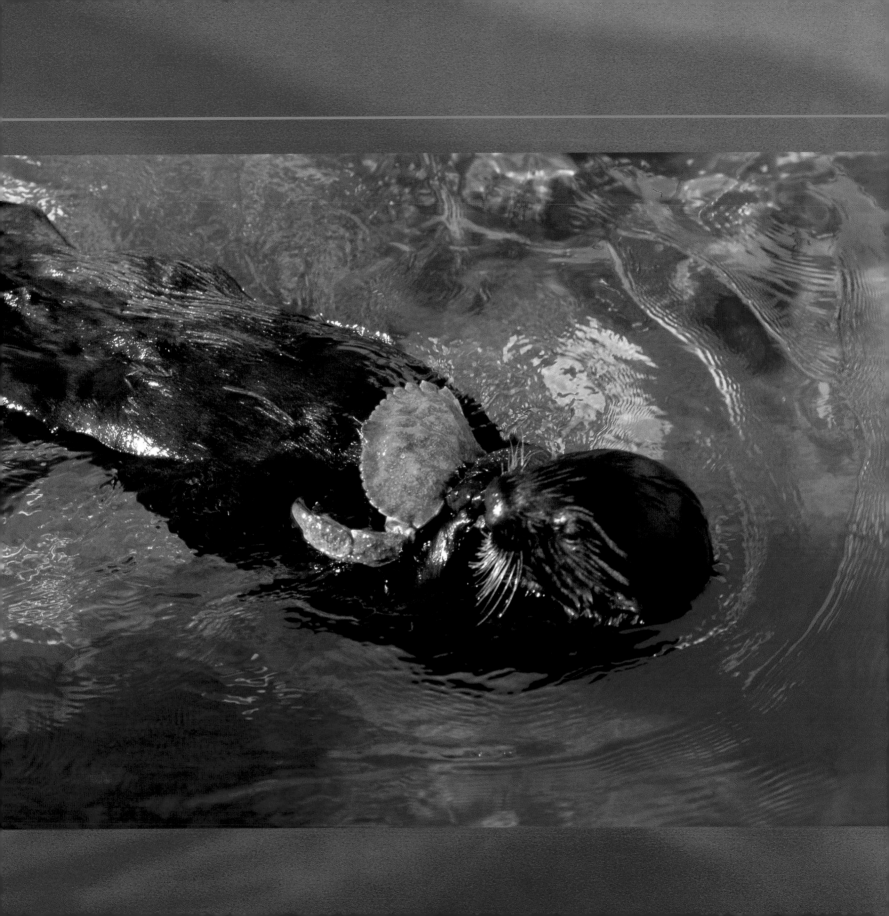

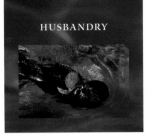

Clamsicles and Hair Clogs

To be honest, the first thing I thought of was the hair. One square inch of a sea otter pup's coat contains ten times the number of hairs on Lady Godiva's entire head. As many as one *million* hairs per square inch! That's got to create a hair clog problem of enormous proportions. But when I pose the question to Candice, she just smiles. Backwashing hair from sand filters is only one of a laundry list of activities that the Monterey Bay Aquarium's rehabilitation staff and volunteers tackle each day. "If you're interested in drain cloggers, scoop your hand in one of those," Candice suggests, motioning toward the blue plastic baskets attached to the drain pipes of each of the sea otter pools in the rehabilitation area. I plunge my hand under water and pull up a glistening collage of purple, gold and indigo—a treasure trove of crab claws, clamshells

◄ *Chronic health problems prevented this female from being reintroduced to the wild. Toys are just one of the many ways SORAC staff provide variety and enrichment to sea otters who will live in an aquarium setting.*

◄▲ *A young sea otter clasps a clamsicle in her flexible paws.*

▲ *A children's slide provides a novel haul-out for this youngster.*

23

▲ *Ice is a favorite treat for aquarium sea otters.*

and smooth ocean rocks. "An otter has to be able to open up a live clam and a good-sized crab before it is eligible for release," she explains. "That takes a lot of practice . . . and creates a real load of debris for our plumbing system to handle."

A high-pitched squeal rises above the gurgle of the water pumps. In less than an instant, a second sea otter takes up the call. With the speed and focus of an experienced day-care worker, Candice hurries from pool to pool dispensing sturdy toy rings, buckets of food and yard-long frozen tubes filled with chunks of clam. "Watch what they do with their clamsicles," Candice whispers. She strides off to deliver a bucket of live food to a sea otter that is slated for release and therefore restricted to an area free from interactions with people.

Straddling her clamsicle like an inflatable beach toy, a seven-month-old sea otter called Thelma (named for a John Steinbeck character, as are most of the SORAC otters) dives beneath the surface and waits patiently for the water pressure to do its work. Each time a piece of clam squirts free from the edge of the tube, Thelma catches it with her paws and stows it away in the loose skin beneath her arms. With her "pockets" well stocked, she returns to the surface to enjoy her feast.

Eddie, on the other hand, employs a more physical approach. Like a superhero, he lifts the tube above his head and sends it crashing against the side of the pool with a resounding "craaaaaack!" A gull swoops down to take advantage of the explosion of clam and ice, but Eddie is too quick to let that happen. Twirling a chunk of clam through his paws like a cob of corn, he backstrokes across the water surface. Four meaty chunks have disappeared down his throat by the time he reaches the far side of the pool.

Sea otters have impressive appetites. A sixty-pound male will consume roughly twenty-five percent of his body weight in clams, crabs, squid and rock cod before the day is through. In the wild, where he will be responsible for not only eating, but also for finding his own food, his daily caloric intake may rise to a whopping 7,000 calories. However much a frustrated dieter might envy this prodigious metabolism, it does come at a cost. A sea otter simply cannot live very long without food. When the storms blow in, or there's a new pup to nurse or when a reliable foraging area has been overfished, the margin for survival grows even slimmer.

To survive in the wild, a rehabilitated sea otter must be able to locate, recognize, capture and ingest a range of prey species in a variety of ocean habitats and weather conditions. The more opportunities a young sea otter has to experience new foods in new circumstances, the better that individual will be equipped to find food upon release. The SORAC staff and volunteers frequently provide the growing pups with kelp, rocks and other common objects from their natural environment. Throughout an average seven-month rehabilitation period, this dedicated team rivals a troupe of Le Cordon Bleu chefs in their pursuit of innovative ways to introduce novel foods. Clamsicles are just one example of this creative spirit at work. Right now, the team is testing an artificial rock outcrop that is loaded with hidden compartments and crevices into which live prey can be stowed.

The selection of prey offered to the rehabilitation sea otters varies with the seasons just as it would in the wild. A peek into the brightly colored laundry baskets that lie submerged in seawater tubs at the back of the food preparation area reveals a smorgasbord of live crabs, clams and mussels. The sight of such

▲ *One look at these rough-housing juveniles and its easy to see why some people call sea otters "kelp grizzlies"!*

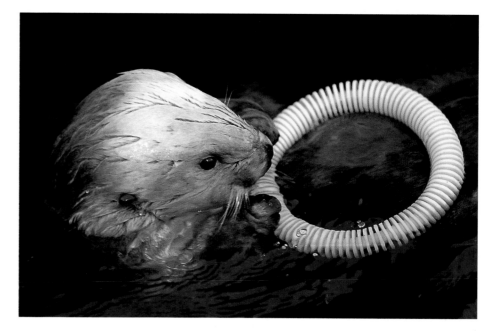

▶ ▶ *Hailey, far right, Roscoe (right) ▶ and Goldie (below), ▼ arrived at the Monterey Bay Aquarium as orphaned pups. Today these permanent residents enjoy a wide variety of toys and favorite foods.*

large, luscious shellfish is enough to set my mouth watering. I make a quick mental note to stop at the local fishmongers to pick something up for dinner. Sea otters will not be the only ones dining on fresh crab tonight. But as I stretch over the side of the tank to help select a suitable candidate for Thelma's noon feeding, Candice mentions how tough it is to get crabs these days. The glorious bounty of California's undersea life is not infinite. Will Thelma be able to find enough food when she is released? Will the West Coast fisheries suffer the same fate as the Grand Banks? Should I be purchasing crabs at this time of year? As the questions turn in my mind, one of the crimson claws clasped between my fingers suddenly shifts and I jerk my hand back from the pinch. Each life touches the other, I think, as I rearrange my grip and follow Candice toward the sea otter area. The survival of each is linked to the survival of the seas.

PUP SWIMS

Diving Buddies

■ The swim program is our best method for increasing their exposure to the natural environment they'll soon re-inhabit.

▲ A pup rests on the chest of a SORAC swimmer, just as it would perch upon its natural mother.

▶ An older pup and diver set out for an ocean swim.

▶▶ Sea stars are just one of a variety of natural objects divers will pick up to show pups during a swim.

Diving Buddies

According to the U. S. Coast Guard, a woman Katie's size would barely last ten minutes if she fell into the North Pacific this time of year. But as Katie is already halfway down the driveway with an eighteen-pound sea otter tucked under her arm, I decide such statistics are best kept to myself. After all, she is fully clothed in a wet suit and has been swimming sea otter pups a whole lot longer than I've been collecting water safety trivia. It's just that the scenario seems somehow backward. A land-based woman is in the midst of taking one of the world's most impressive aquatic mammals out for a swimming lesson.

"Your mistake is thinking of it as a swimming lesson," Katie had tried to explain to me as she was getting suited up for the dive. "A sea otter pup can

◄ *Sea otter pups learn by watching their mothers. Even though this pup is too young to dive, he still keeps a close eye on what the caregiver is doing under water.*

◄▲ *Breath smells are an important way for sea otters to identify each other—and the people who care for them!*

▲ *Pups are so eager to follow under water, they often forget to take a breath!*

float from the moment it's born. Through some marvel of synchronicity, its buoyant baby fur is replaced by a velvet coat that is better for swimming, just at the time the pup develops enough strength and coordination to begin diving under water. Our goal is to swim with the pups as they develop their natural swimming abilities. The swim program is our best method for increasing their exposure to the natural environment they'll soon re-inhabit."

From the moment he touches the water, there is no doubt that Doc knows how to swim. With the undulating body movement of a mermaid, he gracefully powers through the waves. He lazily rolls on to his back and continues his forward movement by alternately pumping his hind flippers. Like diving buddies, Katie and Doc patrol the outer perimeter of a kelp bed, never venturing more than a few yards away from each other's side. With no leash or cord holding the two together, I wonder aloud why Doc does not simply swim off to sea. "He will when he's ready," Sue assures me. "They're like kids in the sense that they each develop differently; they each have their own timing."

Sue has joined me here at the beach at the foot of the Monterey Bay Aquarium to act as a safety spotter for Katie and the pup. I'm delighted to spend more time with her. If there is one thing that I have learned about Sue, it's that she is full of *great* sea otter stories. She got her start in this unusual profession back in 1989, when television news footage of the *Exxon Valdez* oil spill convinced her to go to Alaska to help. She quit her job as a waitress, sold her windsurfer to get enough cash for an airline ticket, participated as a bridesmaid in her sister's wedding and was up in Valdez in less than two weeks. Three months of wet-weather camping and around-the-clock critical care for oiled sea otters were not enough to deter her enthusiasm. When she

◄ *A sea otter pup bobs like a cork thanks to the air trapped in its fluffy "puppy" coat. Until it is shed (at about twelve weeks of age), this built-in life jacket prevents the pup from diving very well.*

▼ *The Monterey Bay Aquarium building was part of John Steinbeck's famous novel* Cannery Row. *Most of the sea otters that enter the SORAC program are given the name of a Steinbeck character.*

▲ *With its close proximity to wild kelp forests and tide pools, the Monterey Bay Aquarium is ideally located for rehabilitating orphaned sea otter pups.*

▶ ▲ *An empty transport kennel on the beach is a good clue that a sea otter and SORAC diver are out for a swim.*

▶ *SORAC divers undergo stringent testing to become certified "otter buddies".*

returned to Monterey, she moved quickly from a volunteer to a staff position within the aquarium's sea otter rehabilitation program.

"Our goal is to have each individual animal succeed in the wild. For some, it happens with the first release, for others it may take more attempts. Whenever I start to get discouraged, I think of a young male sea otter named Joey. His first release was unsuccessful. He came swimming back to the aquarium, squealing for someone to come and pick him up. The second time he was released, he not only came back to the aquarium, he climbed out on the beach and walked all the way back into the building through the shipping and receiving area! But the third release, well, it just clicked. Today he's a wild otter."

The image of a young sea otter calling to be picked up from the beach adjacent to the aquarium sounds like something straight out of a Disney film. But as Sue explains, it's only natural that an animal that's feeling a little vulnerable might return to a place where it has felt safe. A pup involved in the swim program knows this local area better than most, and it is familiar with the route between the beach and the aquarium's rehabilitation area. "One of our greatest challenges," Sue reflects "is providing the pup with all the security it needs as a very young dependent pup, and all the independence it requires as an adult to survive in the wild on its own. That's why we try to move older pups into tanks where the interaction with people is very restricted. Time away from people, often in the company of another sea otter, seems to be an important stage in the transition from a human-focus to a wild-focus."

Clouds are forming across the bay, and as we watch, the wind churns the placid sea into small whitecaps. Katie, who has been warming herself on a rock while Doc was off socializing with a group of wild otters in the kelp, dips back into the choppy sea. She executes a series of slow surface dives and, as if they were partners in a choreographed ballet, Doc follows. Woman and sea otter, each one repeating the other's slow, steady rise and fall. As she resurfaces, Katie offers Doc a live clam from the pouch she's been carrying on her weight belt. "She's trying to help him associate diving with food acquisition," Sue explains. "Can you see what he's doing with his chest?" I borrow her binoculars and watch as Doc swings the clam above his head and bangs it down against the rock balanced on his chest. "He's just starting to get the hang of using a rock to break open the shell. Some sea otters use one rock as a table and another as a hammer. One mother taught her pup to use pop bottles to dislodge mussels from the rock. I've even seen a sea otter wrap itself around a boat buoy to keep from drifting off while it was sleeping. Each develops its own ways of using tools. Young sea otters probably learn these things from their mothers to start with, and that's why we try to give our pups as much exposure to finding and opening food in a typical sea otter habitat as we can."

I watch as a tangle of flippered feet and thick hair swims back toward the beach. It's hard to distinguish where diver ends and sea otter begins. Farther out in the kelp, a mother sea otter is napping. The pup sleeping on her chest is nearly indistinguishable from the mother's thick fur. It doesn't seem possible that these two clingy pups will be living on their own in just a few months time. "The bond is amazingly strong," Sue assures me. "But eventually it breaks. And that's a terrible, wonderful moment."

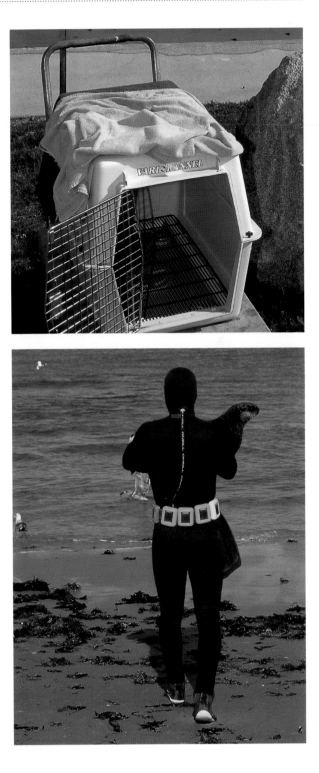

VETERINARY

Minks, Cats, Horses and You!

■ Sea otters have such an interesting mix of characteristics—the kidneys of a sea lion, the loose skin of a hamster and the appetite of a troop of teenaged boys!

▲ Cells from a dead sea otter are harvested to develop a culture for identifying viral infections.

► SORAC veterinarian Dr. Mike Murray specializes in exotic animal medicine, and exotic surgery outfits!

►► Blood samples provide important information about a pup's health status.

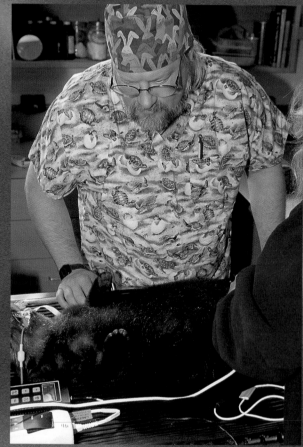

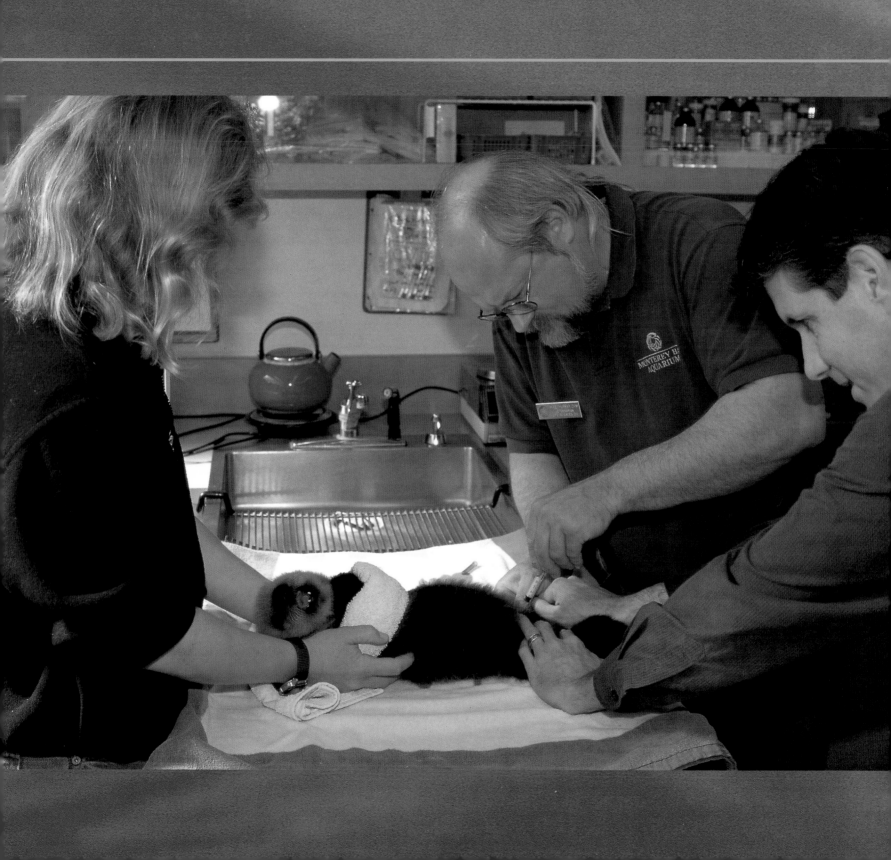

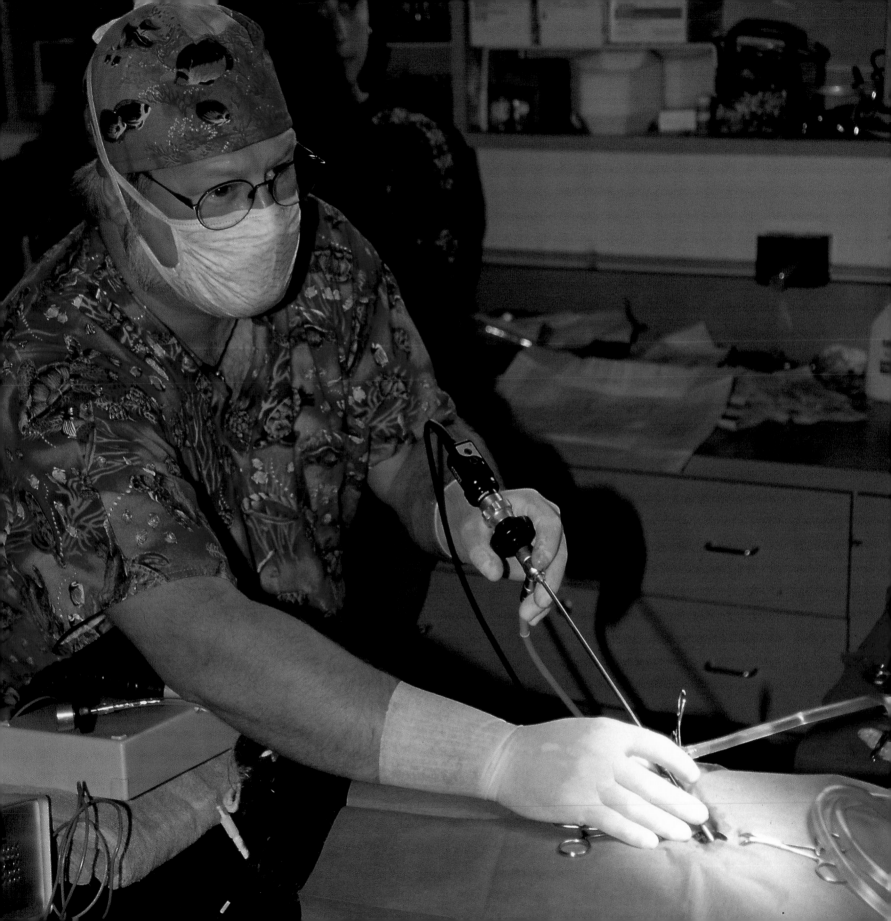

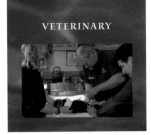

Minks, Cats, Horses and You!

"You've got to admit," Dr. Mike Murray says as we gaze through the nursery window at the pup sleeping on the other side, "they've got a face that lies a bit." My eyes linger over the angelic-looking creature—the same sweet visage that smiles back at me from stuffed toys, greeting cards, coffee mugs and calendars in gift shops the world over. There's no doubt about it; sea otters are cute! However, judging by the thin white scars that line the hands of the SORAC staff, there's another side to the adorable and playful image. "A buzz saw in a fur suit is more like it!" Mike exclaims. "A sea otter is a mustelid, and just like a mink or a badger, it's an animal with an *enormous* attitude. They're not nearly as cuddly as they look."

It's clear how much Mike admires these "weird critters" as he calls them.

◄ *State-of-the-art medical technologies, like this laparoscopic investigation, are essential for diagnosing and treating sick and injured sea otters.*

◄ ▲ *Tissue samples are often sent to a network of medical and research facilities for further analysis.*

▲ *A young sea otter wakes from anesthesia.*

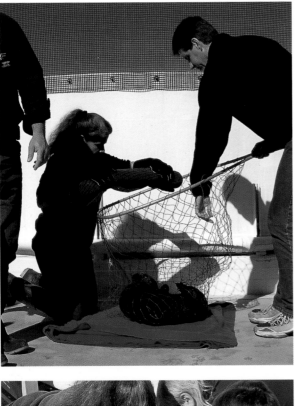

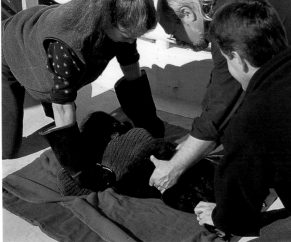

▲ *Welders' gloves and a thick towel provide necessary protection for the caregivers delivering an injection of antibiotics.*

"They've got such an interesting mix of characteristics—the kidneys of a sea lion, the loose skin of a hamster and the appetite of a troop of teenaged boys! Since the early days when SORAC's first veterinarian, Dr. Tom Williams, pioneered orphaned pup care in his home bathtub, we've continued to improve our ability to diagnose why a sea otter is ill and how to care for it. But we're still always learning new things. That's one of the reasons the SORAC program is a success. Not only are more sea otters alive today because of it, but each of these animals has helped us to learn something more about what is 'normal' in terms of sea otter biology."

"When a dog gets sick, a veterinarian has a large body of research literature to draw upon to help determine an accurate diagnosis and treatment. But when you're faced with a sick sea otter, there is no one source of information. You need to look at the published norms for minks, and dogs, and cats and even humans. Take Hunter, for example. We were treating him with a drug to relieve a gastric ulcer. We'd used the drug with other sea otters to great effect, but with Hunter, we discovered a problem with his liver. There was little evidence in the veterinary literature of a connection between this drug and liver problems. But when we looked in the human medicine literature, we found a set of symptoms that matched Hunter's! We took him off the medicine and his liver problem cleared up. So in the course of helping this individual, we learned something important about the possibility of liver function problems with other sea otters."

We stop by the rehabilitation area to check on Summer, a sea otter with damaged fur. "Most mammals are thermally neutral when they're at rest. The body temperature of a harbor seal, for example, remains constant when it's hauled out on a rock. But a sea otter loses heat when it's resting. Sea otters must move or eat to keep warm. And if they're out of the water, they quickly overheat. That's one reason we've got both a heat lamp and a cold water swimming area set up for Summer. She needs to be able to move between the two to maintain her body temperature until her fur improves."

"There are days from hell," Mike confides, as we pause to marvel at a peregrine falcon perched on the disused smoke stack of the old cannery building that is now the aquarium. "There was one day last month when Andy and I had to euthanize two males on the same day. One arrived in an advanced stage of starvation, his teeth too badly worn with age to enable him to feed himself. The other was a younger animal in a coma. He'd suffered a terrible injury that had left half of his skull filled with necrotic tissue. Linda, one of the SORAC staff, cared for the older male through the night, doing her best to make him comfortable, but it was clear that the best thing we could do for both of these animals was to put them down. There was one bright spot on that very sad day, though. We were able to harvest tissues from the males and culture the cells. Today, those cultures are being used to identify viral infections that threaten the wild population."

"Did I tell you my wife plays the bagpipes?" Mike grins, lightening the mood. I watch as he tightens his Hawaiian print surgical cap and bounds down the steps to the surgery. An unstoppable spirit with an affinity for the extraordinary; the aquarium is surely blessed.

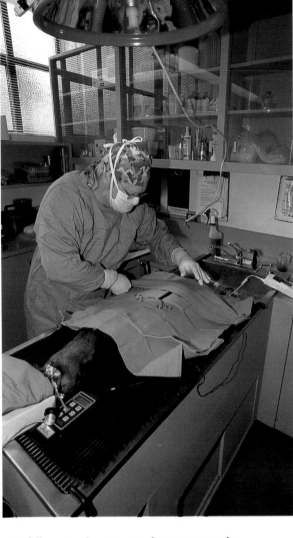

▲ *A fully equipped on-site animal surgery means that sea otters don't need to be transported to other facilities for veterinary care.*

RESEARCH

RELEASE

Alone Again, Naturally

■ The saddest day is the day they arrive at the aquarium—the day they've lost their mothers. But these first few days on their own, these are the scariest.

◄ A SORAC researcher adjusts an antenna to pick up the signal from a sea otter radio transmitter.

▲ Sunrise finds staff already busy netting a juvenile sea otter from an outdoor pool—the first stage in the transportation process that will result in his release.

► A dog kennel lined with ice chips serves as a temporary home during the drive from the aquarium to Elkhorn Slough.

►► The kennel is gently carried along the dock to a waiting boat. A curious harbor dog is not sure what to make of the new arrival.

Alone Again, Naturally

It's June, and for the first time in my life I'm living in California, and I'm wearing long underwear and a fleece jacket. And I'm not alone. All four of the women I've joined on this cliff above Marina State Beach are also wearing fleece . . . and gloves . . . and winter hats. All my images of marine mammal researchers clad only in bathing suits, diving among dolphins in emerald green seas have vanished. Tracking sea otters in the predawn hours is chilly, long, tiring work. But as the gentle conversation that often accompanies such adventures takes hold of the group and the radio transmitter connects with the steady "beep, beep, beep" of a tagged otter's transmitter, the cold is forgotten.

For the next twenty-four hours the radio transmitter—and the spotting scope mounted atop its sturdy tripod—will be our window into the life of a

◄ *Larry White of Monterey Bay Youth donates the use of his boat to transport rehabilitated sea otters to open water release sites.*

◄ ▲ *A SORAC researcher scans the water in search of a suitable release location.*

▲ *Stickers on the back of the radio receiver list frequencies of sea otters tagged by the California Department of Fish and Game and the SORAC program.*

seven-month-old sea otter. A week ago, Bud swam off from Sue during an ocean swim just in front of the Hopkins Marine Station in Pacific Grove. He'd been making longer forays on his own, sometimes staying out at sea for a few hours, sometimes for a few days. But this time, it seems he'd left for good. For seven months, the staff and volunteers of the aquarium's Sea Otter Research and Conservation program had cared for him. From the day they received a call that a newborn sea otter pup was spotted on Pajaro Dunes, until the day he chose to leave, they nursed, groomed, fed and swum him. And now, the goal they committed to when he first entered their program—to rehabilitate him for successful reintroduction back into the rough coastal waters of the Pacific—is being put to a challenging test.

The anticipation is thrilling . . . and frightening. Rehabilitation programs operate in the harsh and sometimes cruel conditions of the natural world. Strong winds have pummeled the coast these past seven days, thwarting earlier efforts to track Bud's progress. Had Bud been able to find food? Could he find tranquil water away from the raging surf? A new wild life is beginning, and I realize why the lawyer in the faded jacket sitting beside me volunteers for the midnight watch even after a busy day in court. And why Michelle, the woman who coordinates the research program, kisses her husband and seven-year-old son goodnight and drives south on Highway 1 through the jet-black night to join us.

The rising sun casts enough light for me to catch the look of concern on Sue's face. When I respond with what I hope is a supportive smile, she murmurs: "The saddest day is the day they arrive at the aquarium—the day they've lost their mothers. But these first few days on their own, these are the scariest."

◄ Elkhorn Slough lies in close proximity to a number of busy harbors but provides calm waters and plentiful food for newly released otters.

▼ One mighty leap and this juvenile male is back in his natural habitat.

TRACKING

Beep, Beep, Beep . . . Beep

■ Radio tags only emit signals when a sea otter is at the surface. So every time an otter dives, you lose both the visual and the auditory clues that mark the animal's whereabouts.

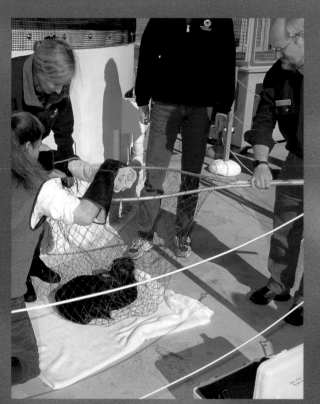

▲ A young male sea otter receives a final health checkup prior to release.

▶ Rather than shaving a patch in a sea otter's coat and exposing the animal to the cold, SORAC staff use lubricating jelly and a cleansing solution to slick down an area of fur in preparation for surgery.

▶▶ An IMAX film crew waits patiently to film a sea otter release.

Beep, Beep, Beep . . . Beep

"Are you sure you'll be home in time for a pancake picnic?" I ask Andy as he loads up his rough weather gear and binoculars. It's July 1, and like many Canadians "living away," I'm looking forward to celebrating Canada Day with a mountain of fried dough and maple syrup. "It shouldn't be any problem," he assures me, closing the trunk of the car. "If the weather gets any windier, we probably won't even be able to get out."

Tracking sea otters by boat always seems to take more time than anticipated. So when 6:00 p.m. comes and goes, I start to feel a little ticked off. He *knows* how much this day means to me! Still, I realize how important it is to try to get a sighting on Eva. Yesterday morning, this seven-month-old female sea otter was released from the SORAC program. But rather than remaining in the

◁ *Trackers often climb to higher altitudes to pick up sea otter radio transmitter signals a mile from shore.*

◁ ▴ *A colorful identification tag is attached like a pierced earring to the webbing between an otter's toes.*

▴ *Southern sea otters have made a remarkable recovery since their near extinction in the late 1800s, but the population is still in peril.*

53

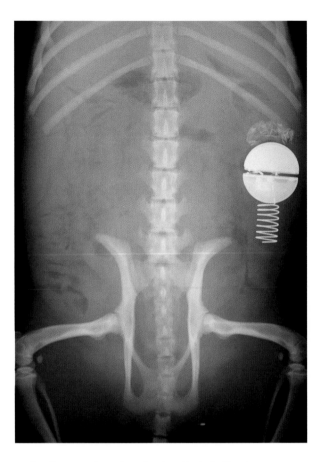

▲ *A radio transmitter about the size of a deck of cards is clearly visible in this x-ray. Long-term studies confirm that the implant does not interfere with a sea otter's health or natural behavior.*

▶ *A faithful dog is good company during the long, long hours of sea otter monitoring.*

quiet waters of Elkhorn Slough, Eva immediately headed out to sea. Bob, the pilot who helps track newly released sea otters by air, picked up Eva's radio signal last night, several miles offshore. The open ocean holds no food or shelter for a sea otter. Under those conditions, she won't survive more than three or four days. The SORAC crew is desperate to get out to reach her.

When 7:00 p.m. passes, a little taste of worry begins to flavor my frustration. The seas are indeed rough and there's no mistaking the small craft warning on the weather channel. By 9:00 p.m., I'm scared. The winds have grown so powerful that the cypress trees bordering the shoreline are twisting back upon themselves like arthritic old ladies. And it's almost dark.

I finish my hundredth long stare through the window, recite my hundredth set of reassurances and have the phone in hand to call the Coast Guard when I hear Andy's footsteps coming up the walk. Hear, that is, the sound of soggy shoes and rain-soaked jeans "squooshing" and "squeeeaaaking" toward our door.

It has been a terribly difficult day. Bob was out early, flying farther and farther from shore toward the location where he left Eva's signal the night before. Andy, Sue, Twyla and Joanne followed behind in a National Oceanic and Atmospheric Administration (NOAA) boat, scanning the water surface with binoculars in the hope of spotting a flash of brown fur. Eight miles off Cypress Point, Bob picks up Eva's signal again. Circling lower for a closer look, he manages to catch sight of her just before she dives under water; a tiny brown speck in an ocean of cold, gray water.

Radio tags only emit signals when a sea otter is at the surface. So every time Eva dives, Bob loses both the visual and the auditory clues that mark her

▶ *Tracking occurs twenty-four hours a day, regardless of weather or location.*

whereabouts. It's a challenging game of hide and seek, made more tense by the grave nature of the game. As hard as it is to see Eva from the air, it's even trickier to catch sight of her from the boat. Thus, as Bob follows Eva from the air, the captain of the boat constantly alters his course in response to Bob's directions from the airplane. All the while, the SORAC team does its best to hold onto their binoculars (and their lunches!) on a roller coaster ride at high sea.

"We were wet from the moment we passed Point Pinos." Andy shivers as he pours water from his left sneaker. "By mile eight the boat was pitching so violently we only managed to catch a glimpse of Eva two or three times. We tried several approaches, but with the waves going one way and the boat going another, there was just no way we could get close enough to catch her in the net. We had to turn back without her."

"Why did Eva swim out to sea?" I ask him. "I wish we knew," he replies.

"But once she stops searching for food and starts swimming, she must keep swimming to stay warm. Eventually, she'll run out of energy. We've got to catch her before she reaches that point."

The following day the seas are still too rough to attempt a return effort by boat. Bob manages to fly over the area when the winds die down in the evening, and against all odds, he picks up Eva's signal! The team is packed and ready to leave at daybreak, but dawn on day three reveals more high winds and stormy seas. Bob stands by, waiting for a shift in the weather. When it finally arrives in the late afternoon, he flies to the location of Eva's last signal. Nothing. He flies ten, twelve, fifteen miles farther off shore. Nothing. With quiet determination he travels thirty miles out to sea and patiently flies a pattern of transect lines across the entire southern sea otter range. Nothing.

It was several weeks later that Andy finished telling me about the return journey. How the rising seas had slowed their forward progress, what it felt like to find themselves in the midst of hundreds of common dolphins, how surprising it was to see solitary sea lions swimming strongly through the foam seven miles from shore, and the excitement on board when two blue whales swam close to the boat. That night, however, worry over Eva's survival overshadowed any joy of seeing wildlife. "Sorry about the pancakes," Andy says, smiling apologetically over a midnight plate of grilled cheese sandwiches. I look across at a man who scaled rocky cliffs in gale force winds to assist Steller sea lion pups, a man who swam day and night in bone-chilling North Pacific waters to help hand-raise a killer whale calf at the Vancouver Aquarium, a man who had to turn back without Eva. "We'll have pancakes another day soon," I answer.

▼ *You need sharp eyes and a good spotting scope to identify the color and placement of a sea otter's tag.*

STRANDINGS

Of Swift Boats and Bloody Noses

■ There's a heightened sense of responsibility when a healthy, young sea otter is injured by people. The SORAC program pledges to facilitate care for every stranded sea otter.

▲ A sea otter on land is not necessarily stranded. This wild adult male often chose to rest on shore.

▶ Female sea otters can incur terrible nose injuries during mating. If the injuries are severe, the female may strand on shore.

▶▶ On the other hand, if a pup this vulnerable and helpless is found on a beach, there is little doubt that it has lost its mother and is badly in need of care.

Of Swift Boats
and Bloody Noses

Mike's been "on his way" to dinner at our house many times but it never seems to happen. Missing dinners is just par for the course for an exotic animal veterinarian. Between laparoscopic examinations of endangered condors and skin treatments for rare lizards, there's little time left for the social pleasantries of life, no matter how tempting. So on New Year's Eve, when we got the call that an injured sea otter was floating near the Coast Guard dock, we knew that same tireless soul would meet us at the aquarium lab for an examination. No matter how late, no matter how often, Mike's there to help. And that's just what you need when you're operating a critical care program for an increasingly threatened population of southern sea otters.

It doesn't take much of an examination to realize that this adult male has

◄ When an ocean storm arises, gale force winds and enormous waves may separate sea otter mothers and pups, leading to pup strandings.

◄◄ Every sea otter released from the SORAC program is given its own individual color combination of flipper tags.

▲ Sea otters live in nearshore waters where they can come into contact with boats. Sometimes collisions occur, causing serious or fatal injuries to the sea otter.

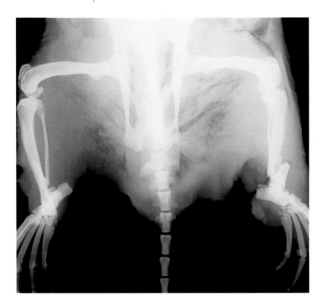

▲ This x-ray image shows the multiple fractures in a sea otter that was hit by a boat.

been clobbered by a boat. Two slices mark a clear trail where the propeller passed over his body. Portable x-rays (developed at 2:00 a.m. by the "Doctors on Duty" staff up the street) confirm fractured ribs, a broken pelvis tip, and fractures to the left lower leg and ankle joint. Luckily, the hit is recent, probably less than twenty-four hours before his discovery. He still has the healthy coat and robust body weight of a healthy adult male.

I watch as Andy gently hands a chunk of ice to the young male: "It's something for him to chomp down on to take his focus off the pain during the intial examination." In this one simple gesture, I am reminded of the questions people often ask about the need for sea otter rehabilitation: "Shouldn't you just leave the animals to die and let nature take its course?" It's a good question, a wise question and one that the members of the SORAC team wrestle with almost daily. The philosophical, ethical and scientific decisions they must make when confronted with a stranded sea otter on a cold, sandy beach are weighed carefully against the specifics of each situation. Is it a pup separated from its mother? Is it an old, emaciated individual missing too many teeth to feed adequately? Is there room in the SORAC facility to care for this animal? Can another facility help? Will bringing this animal to the aquarium impact the resources available to help the others already under care? And always, how might this decision impact the southern sea otter population as a whole? Is it a breeding-age female, for instance, that could produce more pups?

Questioning whether people should interfere with the course of nature is always wise. But to believe that every event that happens in a sea otter's life is natural is to disregard the motor boats, fishing traps, oil leaks and sewage outfalls that are as much a part of their environment as the kelp. There's a heightened sense of responsibility when a healthy, young male sea otter is injured by people. The SORAC program pledges to facilitate care for every stranded sea otter; their involvement was triggered the moment the boat collision occurred.

More than one New Year's has passed since that night. If you happen to find yourself at the Monterey Harbor, keep your eyes open for a male otter sporting orange, pink and brown flipper tags. Thanks to the intricate work of a veterinary orthopedic surgeon and care from the SORAC team, there is one more breeding-age male back in a population that needs all the reproductive success it can muster.

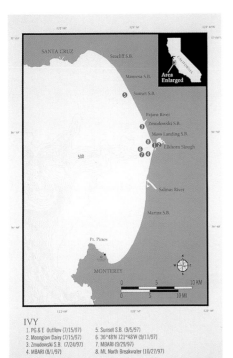

IVY
1. PG & E Outflow (7/15/97)   5. Sunset S.B. (9/5/97)
2. Moonglow Dairy (7/15/97)   6. 36°48'N 121°48'W (9/11/97)
3. Zmudowski S.B. (7/24/97)   7. MBARI (9/29/97)
4. MBARI (8/1/97)   8. ML North Breakwater (10/27/97)

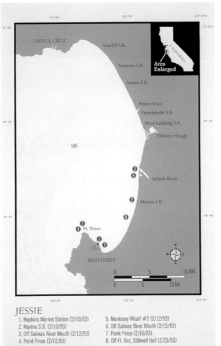

JESSIE
1. Hopkins Marine Station (2/10/93)   5. Monterey Wharf #2 (2/12/93)
2. Marina S.B. (2/10/93)   6. Off Salinas River Mouth (2/15/93)
3. Off Salinas River Mouth (2/12/93)   7. Point Pinos (2/16/93)
4. Point Pinos (2/12/93)   8. Off Ft. Ord, Stillwell Hall (2/23/93)

◄ *Long-term tracking enables researchers to map the movements and habits of individual sea otters in Monterey Bay.*

POSTMORTEMS

Life Lessons

We need to understand the causes of wild sea otter deaths to understand why this threatened population is declining. That's why these necropsies are so important.

A technician prepares a table for a sea otter postmortem.

Rain gear, rubber gloves, rubber boots, plastic aprons . . . SORAC staff help each other into protective clothing before beginning a postmortem.

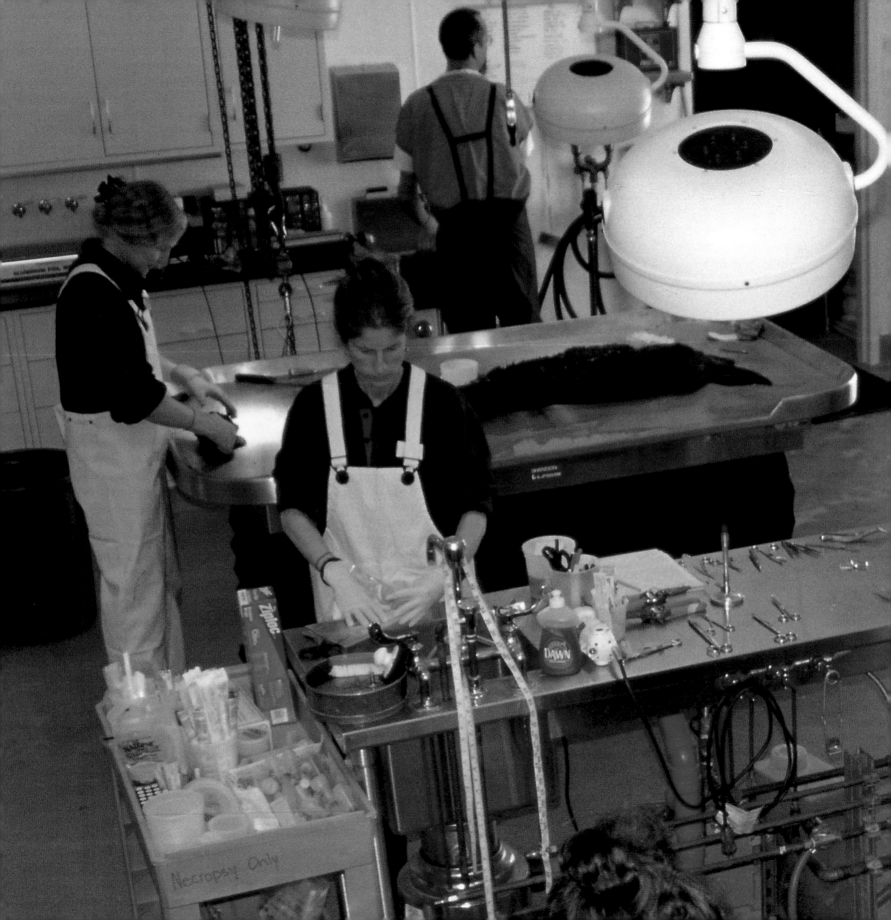

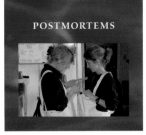

Life Lessons

At first glance, you might think you are standing in a delicatessen. Here are the gleaming metal counters, the plastic containers perched on electronic scales, the white board with instructions for wrapping—foil for this, plastic for that, and whirl packs for anything that needs to be kept frozen. "One of These Nights" from *The Eagle's Greatest Hits* is playing in the tape deck and the room is filled with good-natured banter and the metallic ring of utensils on tables.

But this is not a deli. It's the postmortem lab at the Marine Wildlife Veterinary Care and Research Center in Santa Cruz, California. And the individuals chatting amiably over tables are not diners, but sea otter researchers and veterinary pathologists. They've gathered to perform necropsies on fourteen dead sea otters found along the central California coast during the

◄ *Instruments and containers to collect specimens are laid out in preparation for a postmortem on a sea otter found dead on a local beach.*

◄▲ *The southern sea otter population is declining across all age classes. That means that the chances of a mother dying are just as great as that of her pup.*

67

MUSCLES	LYMPH NODES	FOIL	CONTENTS
-MASSETER	tag, measure, weigh	-BRAIN (1)	-STOMACH
-TEMPORAL	L & R where applicable	-SKEL MUSC. (1)	
-VENTRAL NECK	-SUBMANDIBULAR	-SKIN (1)	-PROX INT.
-INTERCOSTAL	-RETROPHARYNGE	-LIVER (2-3)	
-DIAPHRAGM	-PRESCAPULAR	-KIDNEY (2-3)	-DISTAL INT.
-PROX. F LIMB	-AXILLARY	-FAT (1)	-FECES
-PROX. R LIMB	-HILAR/PERI BRONCHIAL		
	-MESENTERIC	WHIRL-PAKS	
	-INGUINAL-	-SKEL MUSC. (1)	
	-SUBLUMBAR	-LIVER (3)	
	-POPLITEAL	-KIDNEY (3)	
		-SPLEEN (1)	
OTHER		-LUNG (1)	
Measure & weigh	CASSETTES		
-THYROID	-PITUITARY	FLUIDS	
-THYMUS		-CSF	
-ADRENAL	SWABS	-BILE	
	-HEART BLOOD/SPLEEN	-URINE	
	-LOWER GI	-SERUM (SPIN FROM CHICKEN FAT CLOT)	
		-CHEST FLUID	

SSO NEC LIST

▲ *A white-board sign reminds staff and volunteers how various tissue samples must be collected and stored.*

past two weeks. Some of the animals were collected and stored in freezers by California Department of Fish and Game or Monterey Bay Aquarium staff; individuals patrolling beaches as part of a regional marine mammal stranding network found others. While most of the bodies arrive in large picnic coolers, a few come by courier, courtesy of Federal Express!

Like members of a quilting bee, everyone seems to know their role and position around the table. A quick step into a pair of yellow rubber overalls and the donning of green rubber gloves is a signal for work to begin. "I've got a bunch of one pagers here," Jack shouts, referring to sea otters that are small enough to fit on one sheet of x-ray film. A bright spot on an x-ray is an efficient way to see if an otter sustained a gun shot. "How fresh are they?" Michelle asks, tugging at the hair on three pups laid out before her. "Fresh" means an animal that died close to the time it was discovered. The hair on fresh animals is still firmly attached to the skin. Because it's fresh, one of the three animals is saved for a pathology examination. The others are carefully measured and then placed in the bin for disposal.

"That's an old lady, look at her teeth!" Mike peers into the open mouth and then stretches out the flippers on her hind feet to reveal a mosaic of bite marks and scars. A healed triangular scar covers most of the nose pad, a testament to previous mating episodes. "When the bones are so awfully prominent, and there's so little muscle, you can tell she was in very poor shape when she died," he explains.

Dr. Nancy Kock, a pathologist who recently moved to the area from Zimbabwe where her patients were just as likely to be hippos as lions, tosses a tiny tape recorder into the opening of a surgical glove and with glove to lip, commences her commentary. "A mammal is a mammal is a mammal," she says as she carefully cuts open the body cavity. With amazing skill and precision, she snips and slices tiny samples from each of the major organs, muscles and vessels. As Nancy cuts, Erin packages. Lymph nodes pegged on laundry tags are marked and dropped into tubs of formalin. Kidneys are wrapped in foil and plastic and stored at -70 degrees Fahrenheit. Blood that will be spun to produce serum is transferred from a large syringe to a waiting plastic bag. The value of the serum to a Ph.D. student's research study is clear. Written in bold on the necropsy checklist is a promise that, "For every 'fresh dead' otter you get more than 1 cc 'serum' from, I will personally make brownies or cookies!"

"Every organ has a variety of lesions that are typical for it. That's what you look for," Nancy tells me as she works systematically through the body. She picks up a saw and makes a clean cut through a rib. "This bone is soft, which is another sign that the animal was unhealthy when it died. Younger bones are soft too, but in a different sort of way. And the bones of a healthy adult are strong and much more difficult to cut." Karl, a research student, stops by the table and makes a request for the entire digestive tract. He needs it for his study of parasitic worms. Karl's research is timely given the recent increase of deaths from intestinal parasites in the sea otter population.

I look across to another table where Michelle and Mike are working on a mature female sea otter. "Oh no," Michelle exclaims as she carefully lifts a tiny, perfectly formed fetus from its dead mother. We examine the petite nails, the silky soft whiskers, the gently rounded paws. Fourteen sea otter deaths have become fifteen and we are that much sadder to bear witness to it.

▼ *This sea otter appears healthy, yet detailed postmortems reveal that approximately forty percent of southern sea otter deaths are disease-related.*

SCIENTIFIC STUDY

Old Dogs, Young Women and the Midnight-to-Midnight Shift

■ For the first time, researchers are able to compare the behavior and survivorship of wild pups raised by their mother's with rehabilitated pups raised by the SORAC team.

▲ Dr. Dave Jessup of California Department of Fish & Game examines a female otter.

▶ A research boat prepares to return a wild sea otter mother and pup to sea.

▶▶ A young male squeals in surprise at being photographed during a harmless research trial. Within the safety of a SORAC tank young sea otters nearing release help scientists study the behavior of these animals around fish traps.

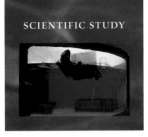
Old Dogs, Young Women and the Midnight-to-Midnight Shift

It must be a strange sight for the tourists. The blood sample is being drawn under the awning of a rather ordinary looking RV. It's a warm spring day and the Coast Guard pier where we're parked is crowded with scuba divers and families enjoying ice cream cones. A woman pushing a stroller stops to watch as Michelle and Twyla sort through a pile of brightly colored flipper tags they've spread out on the pavement before them. "Otter jewelry," Michelle teases as she swiftly clips an orange tag through the webbing on the sea otter's hind foot. "See, it's like putting on an earring," the mother explains to the toddler. "Every time they see the orange tag, they'll know which otter this is."

It's taken less than five minutes for the team to weigh, flipper tag and draw blood samples from the female sea otter. Little more than half an hour ago, she

◀ *Researchers rely on advanced diving technology to enable them to sneak up on sea otters from below the kelp canopy.*

◀▲ *This camper van has been transformed into a portable veterinary unit for wildlife research studies.*

▲ *Wilson traps offer a safe and humane way to trap wild mother-pup pairs for sea otter research.*

73

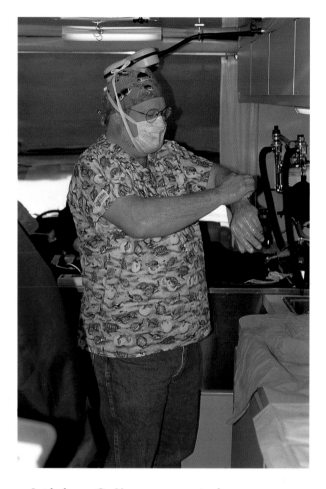

▲ *Inside the van, Dr. Murray prepares to implant a radio transmitter into a wild sea otter pup.*

and her pup were resting in the kelp bed just off Point Pinos. Now, as she waits in an ice-cube laden kennel for transport back to sea, Mike and a team of wildlife biologists are inside the trailer performing surgery on her pup. This is no ordinary RV after all. The interior is a high-tech animal surgery unit capable of supporting veterinary procedures in remote locations. Mike makes a small incision in the pup's abdomen and gently inserts a radio transmitter. It's an operation he's performed dozens of times and his experience shows. The pup is out from under the anesthetic and back in the kennel with her mother just an hour and a half after the initial capture took place.

"This is an unprecedented research study," Dr. Jim Estes, from the University of California, Santa Cruz, tells me as we watch Michelle and Twyla carry the kennel down the pier and lift it onto the floor of an inflatable motor boat. "The southern sea otter population is declining, and we need to find out what happens to pups during their first years of life. For the first time, we'll be able to compare the behavior and survivorship of wild pups raised by their mothers with rehabilitated pups raised by the SORAC team. It's exactly the kind of study that is so badly needed."

I perch beside Michelle as we head toward the kelp. She is a very attractive woman, but at this moment, as she powers the boat through the swells, her hair blowing wildly behind her, she has the determined look of the Wicked Witch of the West in hot pursuit of Dorothy. She is a woman with a mission: a mission to get a mother sea otter and her pup back out to sea.

We reach the kelp bed where the pair was originally captured. The kennel is opened and within seconds, we hear two large "plops!" as sea otters and water reunite. The mother surfaces on one side of the boat, the pup on the other, and there are a few tense moments as the pair appear to be heading off in separate directions. Michelle puts her fingers to her lips and makes a shrill whistle; the mother otter responds to the whistle with her own call and within seconds, her pup squeals in return. We hold our breath as the mother speeds toward her daughter. Like a cat carrying a nearly grown kitten, the mother sea otter grabs her pup by the scruff of its neck and hoists it up onto her chest. For the next ten minutes, every inch of the pup's coat is thoroughly rubbed, scrubbed and fluffed, the mother pausing now and then to blow air into the rapidly drying fur.

Michelle pulls the boat away slowly, relieved to see the pup resting peacefully at the surface while its mother begins diving for food. This is the third mother-pup pair the team has handled today, and everyone is tired. Yet, for Krista, the woman responsible for the study, the work has just begun. For the rest of today and throughout the next few weeks, she and many of the SORAC staff and volunteers will monitor each of the pairs. They'll be watching to make sure there are no post-surgical complications and to try to pinpoint the date of weaning. The team will monitor each wild pup for a full two years post-weaning, just as they do each sea otter released from the SORAC program.

That night, as I cycle home in the dark along the recreation trail that hugs the coastline of Monterey Bay, I spot Krista's tracking vehicle pulled off to the side of the road. Two old dogs lie comfortably sprawled on the tarmac, soaking up heat trapped in the pavement from the afternoon sun. I hear the transmitter signal and catch a glimpse of two young silhouettes patrolling the beach with aerial in hand. Vigils come in many forms: old dogs watching over young women, young women watching over sea otters—expressions of care extended through the night while most of us lie snug in our beds.

▼ *A boat returns the mother-pup pair to the kelp forest where they were originally captured. Total time elapsed? Two hours.*

CONSERVATION

AQUARIUM HOMES

Tarmac Farewells

■ There will always be a few sea otters that for health or behavioral reasons won't succeed in the wild. Aquarium exhibits provide healthy homes and promote public education and captive breeding.

◄ A mother sea otter gently sculls with her hind flippers, her young pup firmly cradled beneath her left paw.

▲ (above) and (right) ► Staff and volunteers at the Long Marine Lab worked tirelessly to train these sea otters to feel comfortable during their transport to a Colorado aquarium.

►► A hose connected to the van's air-conditioning unit prevents this male sea otter from overheating during transit.

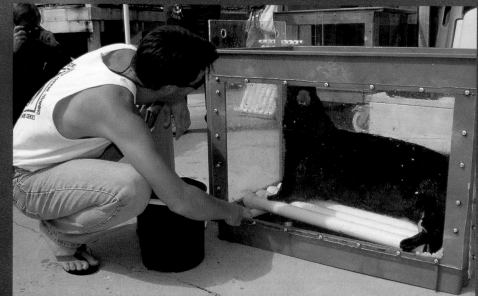

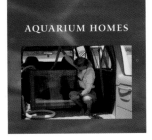

Tarmac Farewells

It has all the signs of a rock star send off. A private jet stands on the runway of an airport in central California. An unmarked van with tinted windows pulls up, the driver hops out and swiftly transfers a copious amount of luggage from the van to the cargo portion of the plane. Moments later, a second, third and fourth vehicle arrive. Doors open simultaneously and ten long-haired women in their early twenties step down upon the tarmac. Dressed in flip-flops and blue jeans, they huddle together in an emotional embrace. It's time to say goodbye.

When the air-conditioning in the van is finally switched off and the passenger doors are opened, the faces that emerge could never be called famous. Yet, there's little doubt they could charm even the most cynical paparazzi. Taylor and Gracie emerge with a noisy fanfare of squeals and

◄ *With the transport kennel firmly secured, SORAC staff prepare for take-off.*

◄ ▲ *Sea otters are transported in small private planes to ensure a fast, direct route to their new homes.*

▶ *Saying good-bye to a sea otter you've cared for is never an easy thing.*

high-pitched whistles. Sea otters don't usually travel by van or by airplane, and it's obvious these two young adults are not feeling entirely comfortable with the journey thus far.

"It's been more than a year since we took over the care of these two from the SORAC program, and I'm sure it'll help to have a familiar person traveling with them," Heather explains. "Luckily we know Pete and the others who'll be looking after them at Colorado's Ocean Journey, so we know they'll be in good hands." Heather's upbeat manner is not matched by her teammates, who are sadly clicking pictures of their departing charges. For the past year, these young students from the University of California Santa Cruz have each volunteered fifteen to twenty hours a week to clean pools, prepare food and generally make life more interesting for the sea otters that are now boarding the jet. "We know it's the best thing that could happen for them, but that doesn't make saying good-bye one bit easier."

A few years ago, a trip like this would rarely have happened. Since the SORAC program began in the mid-1980s, there have always been a few animals that for health or behavioral reasons just haven't succeeded in the wild. For a number of years those animals were cared for in the behind-the-scenes area of the Monterey Bay Aquarium. But the situation wasn't ideal. The rehabilitation facilities were not designed as long-term living areas for sea otters. Also, these "non-releasable" animals took valuable space and staff time away from the stranded animals the program was designed to serve, and the "off exhibit" status of the animals meant that the aquarium's commitment to public education was not being accomplished. "For every sea otter, there's a mile of red tape," a Fish and Game representative told me a few days ago. "The restrictions are there to protect this threatened species. But in this case, that red tape was preventing non-releasable sea otters from being housed in public exhibits at other aquariums where their needs for space and attention would be much better met, and the goals of public education and captive breeding could be realized."

Until the SORAC program developed this collaborative process, the way many aquariums acquired sea otters for public display was to capture them from the wild. This is illegal in the case of the southern sea otter population, but there are still aquariums operating today that will spend $250,000 to purchase a pair of sea otters collected from the northern population. It's taken a lot of effort by many agencies, but, by the year 2000, eight aquariums across North America will exhibit southern sea otters from our SORAC program.

Heather pours chipped ice into Taylor and Gracie's kennels as the jet engines prepare for take-off. By now, all of the women on the tarmac are wearing sunglasses, despite the overcast state of the day. Sunglasses are ideal for hiding tears. It's hard to say farewell to good friends, even when they're already celebrities elsewhere.

▼ *By the year 2000, eight North American aquariums will exhibit non-releasable southern sea otters from the SORAC program.*

LIVING WILD

In The Company of Wild Otters

▲ Boats are requested to stay at least fifty feet away from a sea otter to prevent disturbing their natural behavior. Too often, people ignore this rule, interfering with an already threatened population of sea otters.

▶ "Thwack, thwack, thwack!" A sea otter hoists a clam above its head and repeatedly sends it cracking down upon the rock balanced on its chest. Each sea otter has its own preferred way of opening tough shells.

■ When a sea otter is released, SORAC staff and volunteers track its progress, recording all of its activities for the first twenty-four hours. These observations are repeated every two months for the next two years—or longer if the transmitter battery holds out!

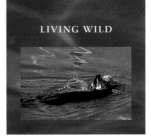

In the Company of Wild Otters

It could just as easily have been a conversation at a high school reunion. "Look, there's Harmony and Ivy, but who are they with? I don't recognize him, do you?" Michelle and Sue lean forward for a better view. "Did I tell you Rice is in the area?" Michelle mentions casually. "Rice! Really, Rice? I'd love to see Rice. He was the cutest, he looked just like a muppet and I haven't seen him in ages!" "Wait, there's Morgan." Sue's attention is diverted by another long-lost love several yards away. "Are you sure it's him?" Michelle whispers. "Yep," Sue replies, her eyes twinkling. "I can see his pink tag."

As many as eighty sea otters have been sighted in Elkhorn Slough. As we slowly motor through this narrow, winding waterway, I grow increasingly convinced that Michelle and Sue know all of them. Michelle laughs at my

◀ *The sea otter in the center has lived its whole life in the wild. The other two were raised by SORAC as orphaned pups. This is just the kind of social integration the program seeks to achieve.*

◀▲ *A sea otter pup receives constant grooming, feeding, attention and training from its mother. The task is incredibly demanding. Single births are the norm, twins a rarity.*

▲ *Sea otter whiskers are as stiff as a monofilament fishing line, yet sensitive enough to detect the movement of prey.*

suggestion. "When I was out eight hours a day, several days per week as a research assistant, I could recognize more than twenty-five sea otters by sight. But I'm not out as often now that I'm coordinating the research program." Maybe so, but she still identifies an old grizzled male as #718 without a second thought. "Rice, Morgan, Harmony and Ivy were all sea otters that came through the SORAC program. That's why they look so familiar. And, besides," Sue smiles, holding up an antenna that looks like something you'd find on your grandmother's television, "we've been tracking them by their transmitters!"

SORAC's commitment to the long-term monitoring of every sea otter they reintroduce is rare among rehabilitation programs. When a sea otter is released, SORAC staff and volunteers track its progress, recording all of its activities for the first twenty-four hours. This period is followed by two solid weeks of observations during daylight hours. Then a second, around-the-clock, intensive monitoring session is conducted. These twenty-four-hour observations are repeated every two months for the next two years—or longer if the transmitter battery holds out!

It doesn't take a mathematician to recognize the amount of time such intense monitoring demands. What it does take is individuals willing to volunteer untold hours to cover late-night treks along the seashore and early morning shifts in the slough. Somewhere between board meetings and school lunches, these volunteers have squeezed a little more wildness into their lives than the rest of us. When they describe what it feels like to watch a newly weaned pup survive its first storm, or to discover a sea otter from the SORAC program sleeping alongside two wild otters in the kelp, you sense they're all the richer for having glimpsed it.

Serving witness to the trials of a newly released sea otter exacts a heavy toll on the people involved. The first two weeks that a young sea otter spends on its own, whether having just weaned from its mother or from the care of the SORAC team, are among the riskiest days in its life. "Yet, in your heart," Michelle tells me, "you carry an unrealistic hope that every animal you release will survive. Even though we know that some will die, it doesn't make it any easier when an animal you've nurtured runs into difficulties." As one volunteer so eloquently phrased it: "There is still so much pain in the joy of this work."

◄ *With a graceful arch of its back and a powerful kick of its back flippers, a sea otter glides through the water like an aquatic dancer.*

▼ *Sea otters are currently listed as a "threatened species" under the U.S. Endangered Species Act. Can they be saved?*

When a rehabilitated animal appears to be having trouble, it's always difficult to decide whether intervening would be helpful or hurtful to its long-term integration into the wild. "There's real tension when we meet as a group to decide how we should proceed," Sue confides. "No matter how much we wish such a thing existed, there is no definitive reference to tell us what to do. Each case is unique, and each of us brings our own experiences, personal feelings and academic backgrounds to the table. We come in with information based on many years of collecting scientific data from previous releases and leave with a consensus plan. But it's never easy."

This willingness to participate in difficult decisions, to pioneer techniques that no one has tried before, and to proceed as if it is possible to save southern sea otters has earned SORAC high respect within the conservation and research community. This past year, when El Niño storms wreaked havoc on the Pacific coastline, catapulting fifty percent more sea otters into SORAC care than any other year previously, the staff and volunteers worked double time, and sometimes triple time, to meet the demand. Thankfully, the effort was rewarded. In this, its busiest year to date, the SORAC program enjoyed a 100 percent increase in survivorship over the previous year.

The boat draws closer toward three adult sea otters lounging in the warmth of the midday sun. An unknown wild otter lies sandwiched between Harmony and Ivy.

"Saving southern sea otters is such a demanding goal, you have to try to see successes each step of the way," Michelle tells me. "Harmony came to us at five weeks of age. She was the youngest pup we ever raised in a tank without

human contact; she and Ivy grew up together as tankmates. I remember watching her catch crabs in the pickleweed the first three weeks after her release. I remember how Ivy would spend her days offshore, only returning to the slough to feed each night. And, I'll never forget those midnight monitoring shifts at the dairy by the slough listening to the sound of their transmitters with nothing but the smell of the barnyard to keep me awake! But today, they're living in the company of wild sea otters."

"Just as it should be," Sue chimes in. Just as it should be, indeed.

▲ *A "raft" of sea otters looks up from the kelp. Sometimes juvenile males raft together; other rafts are comprised of mothers, pups and a territorial male.*

CONCLUSION

If you're lucky enough to find yourself on the Monterey Peninsula on a clear summer's eve, take yourself down to the seashore. As the sun spreads long and low across the horizon, every wave, every stone, every blade of kelp is transformed into a glittering tapestry of gold. The once cool gray waters gleam with the brilliance of molten lava; the sun-kissed wake of a lone sea otter etches a thin, white line across the sea's metallic surface.

It is possible at moments like these to understand passion for marine conservation. In the presence of such beauty, a commitment to save southern sea otters and the rich diversity of the Pacific Ocean is difficult to question. But the challenge of saving sea otters extends far beyond these ethereal encounters.

During the months that I shadowed the SORAC staff and volunteers, observing their daily activities and sharing their frustrations, hopes and aspirations, it became obvious that sea otter conservation demands much more than a love for the sea or the critical care of orphaned

animals. It's a complicated quest that cannot be accomplished alone. When speeding boats in and around Elkhorn Slough caused four sea otter deaths over a nine-month span, including two rehabilitated animals from the SORAC program, the SORAC team convened a meeting of all of the agencies and individuals involved with boat traffic and sea otter conservation in the area. The resulting multi-group task force is now actively engaged in resolving the problem of speeding in the slough. Similarly, when evidence from both California and Alaska revealed accidental sea otter deaths from drowning in fish traps, the SORAC program joined forces with university and government scientists to discover how sea otters behave around fish traps and what trap modifications could prevent sea otter mortalities. Meetings with politicians, environmental groups, fishermen, kayak rental companies, scientists, government agencies . . . saving southern sea otters requires ongoing collaborative relationships with a vast array of individuals, many of whom hold competing visions of what constitutes progress and success.

I am pondering the enormity of this challenge when Andy's pager goes off. Pippin, a young female sea otter is en route from the Marine Mammal Center in Sausalito to the SORAC program. After checking the page for her estimated time of arrival, Andy puts in a quick call to the aquarium's public relations department. An Imax film crew is currently on-site working on a segment about the SORAC program, and the media staff are eager to alert them to Pippin's arrival. "We'll have to play it by ear," Andy cautions. "If she appears to be very nervous, we'll have to limit access to just the SORAC staff." An Imax film brings with it the promise that millions of viewers will better understand, and, hopefully, become more commited to the survival of sea otters. But at this moment, the value of a film shoot takes second seat to the requirements of a frightened orphaned pup. "It seems like we're always balancing the needs of an individual animal with the needs of the sea otter population overall," Andy tells me as he grabs his bike lock and heads for the door. Their survival ultimately depends on how well we meet the needs of both."

Published in the United States by the Monterey Bay
Aquarium Foundation, 886 Cannery Row, Monterey, CA
93940-1085 http://www.mbayaq.org

Printed on recycled paper and bound in Hong Kong by
Global Interprint
9 8 7 6 5 4 3 2 1

PHOTO CREDITS: All photos by Doc White, except photographs
by Richard Bucich: 58 (left); Melissa Chechowitz & Linda
Lowenstine: 62; Andrew Johnson/Monterey Bay Aquarium:
9 (bottom left), 36 (top left), 38, 39 (inset and bottom right),
44 (bottom right), 51, 52, 55, 56, 61 (inset), 64-66, 68, 70, 72-75,
78-82, 84, 89, 92-93, 94, back cover flap; Monterey Bay
Aquarium: 54, 63; Steven Webster: 60.

Design: Elizabeth Watson
Publisher: Nora L. Deans
Project Editors: Roxane Buck-Ezcurra and Michelle McKenzie

◄ Page 94: You can walk many miles in response to a report
of a sea otter stranding. In this case, the sea otter was
eventually spotted from a hang glider!